EDGE OF MEDICINE

TRANSPLANT BREAKTHROUGHS

HEATHER E. SCHWARTZ

MAYO CLINIC PRESS KIDS

To Philip, Jaz, and Griffin

MAYO CLINIC PRESS KIDS | An imprint of Mayo Clinic Press
200 First St. SW
Rochester, MN 55905
mcpress.mayoclinic.org
To stay informed about Mayo Clinic Press, please subscribe to our free e-newsletter at mcpress.mayoclinic.org or follow us on social media.

Published in the United States by Mayo Clinic Press Kids, an imprint of Mayo Clinic Press.

ISBN: 978-1-945564-83-3 (paperback) | 978-1-945564-84-0 (library) | 978-1-945564-85-7 (ebook) | 979-8-88770-090-8 (multiuser PDF) | 979-8-88770-089-2 (multiuser ePub)

Library of Congress Control Number: 2022942578
Library of Congress Cataloging-in-Publication Data is available upon request.

TABLE OF CONTENTS

SECOND CHANCES AND SAVING LIVES

In 2021, 57-year-old David Bennett lay in a hospital bed dying of heart disease. By February 2022, he was sitting up watching the Super Bowl on television. Bennett visited with family and thought about getting home to see his dog, Lucky. It seemed his life had been saved.

Bennett had received a new heart. He had also made history. He was the first person to receive a pig heart rather than a human heart. Bennett's **surgery** inspired doctors. It made a huge impact on the organ transplant field by offering a new way to help future patients. And it was just one transplant breakthrough!

Surgeons and inventors build on decades of research to explore new transplant methods and technologies. Because of these advancements, many transplant recipients live longer, healthier lives. Organ transplants save and improve thousands of lives each year.

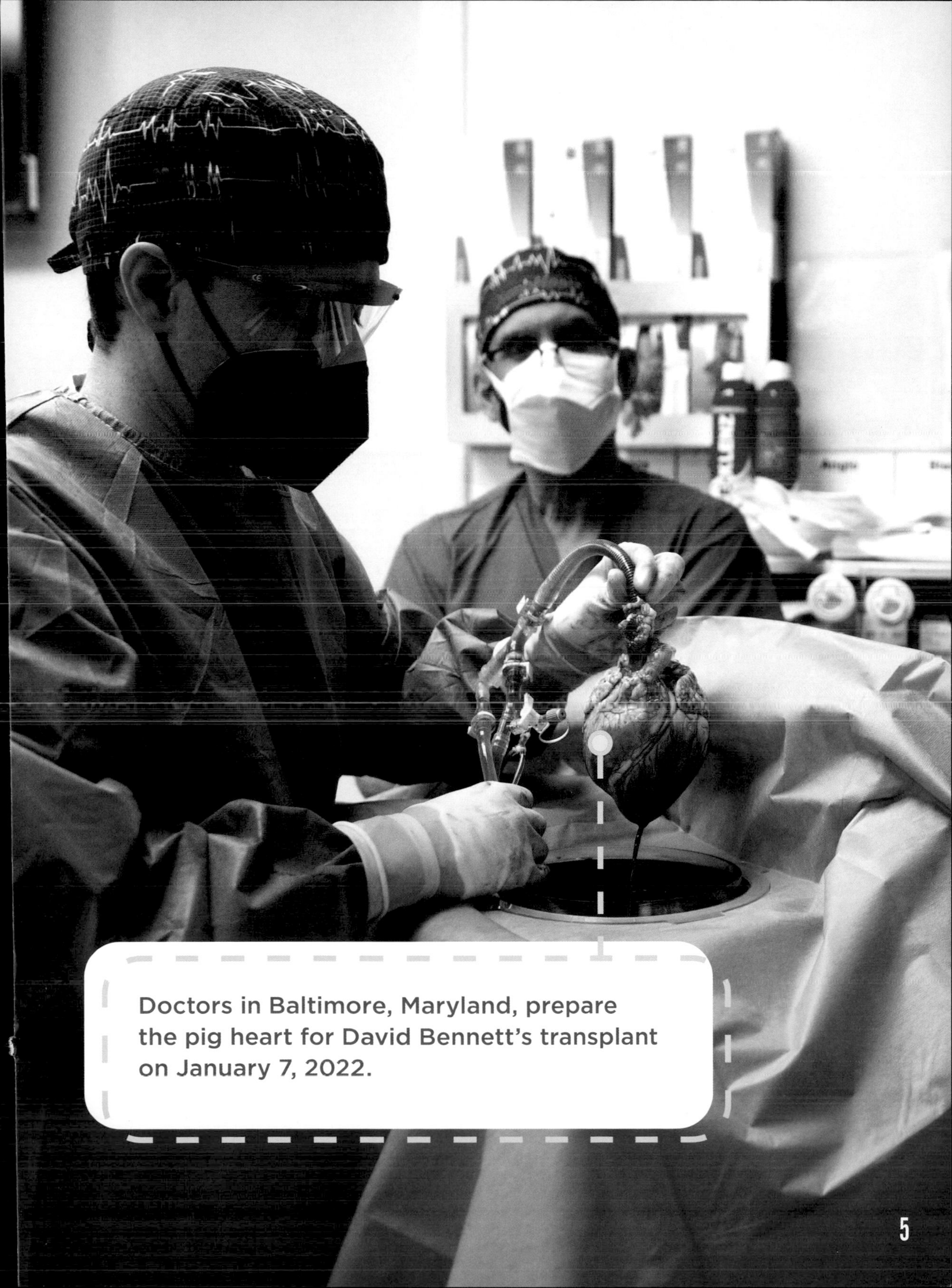

Doctors in Baltimore, Maryland, prepare the pig heart for David Bennett's transplant on January 7, 2022.

EARLY EYE TRANSPLANTS

In the 1830s, Irish surgeon Samuel Bigger thought **corneal** transplant might cure blindness. He tested his idea on animals. Bigger transplanted a gazelle cornea into a blind gazelle's eye. The surgery worked! This led US doctor Richard Kissam to wonder if an animal cornea could be transplanted into a human eye.

In 1838, Kissam transplanted a pig cornea into a young man's eye. The transplant allowed the man to see some light. But within two weeks, he was blind again. Still, Kissam's transplant broke new ground. It was the first corneal transplant performed on a human!

Kissam's surgery was just one example of using animal organs in transplant experimentation. Exploring medical practices on animals is **controversial**. Some people feel it is unfair to animals. Others believe it is a good way to make discoveries. Kissam's surgery drove doctors to further study corneal transplants.

In 1905, Austrian doctor Eduard Zirm attempted history's second corneal transplant. Instead of an animal donor, Zirm received the cornea from a young boy. Though the boy's cornea was intact, the rest of his eye was damaged and not functional. The boy's father allowed Zirm to remove the eye.

Zirm transplanted the cornea into the eye of a man who had been blinded by burns. The transplant worked! The man could see again, and his sight was **permanent**.

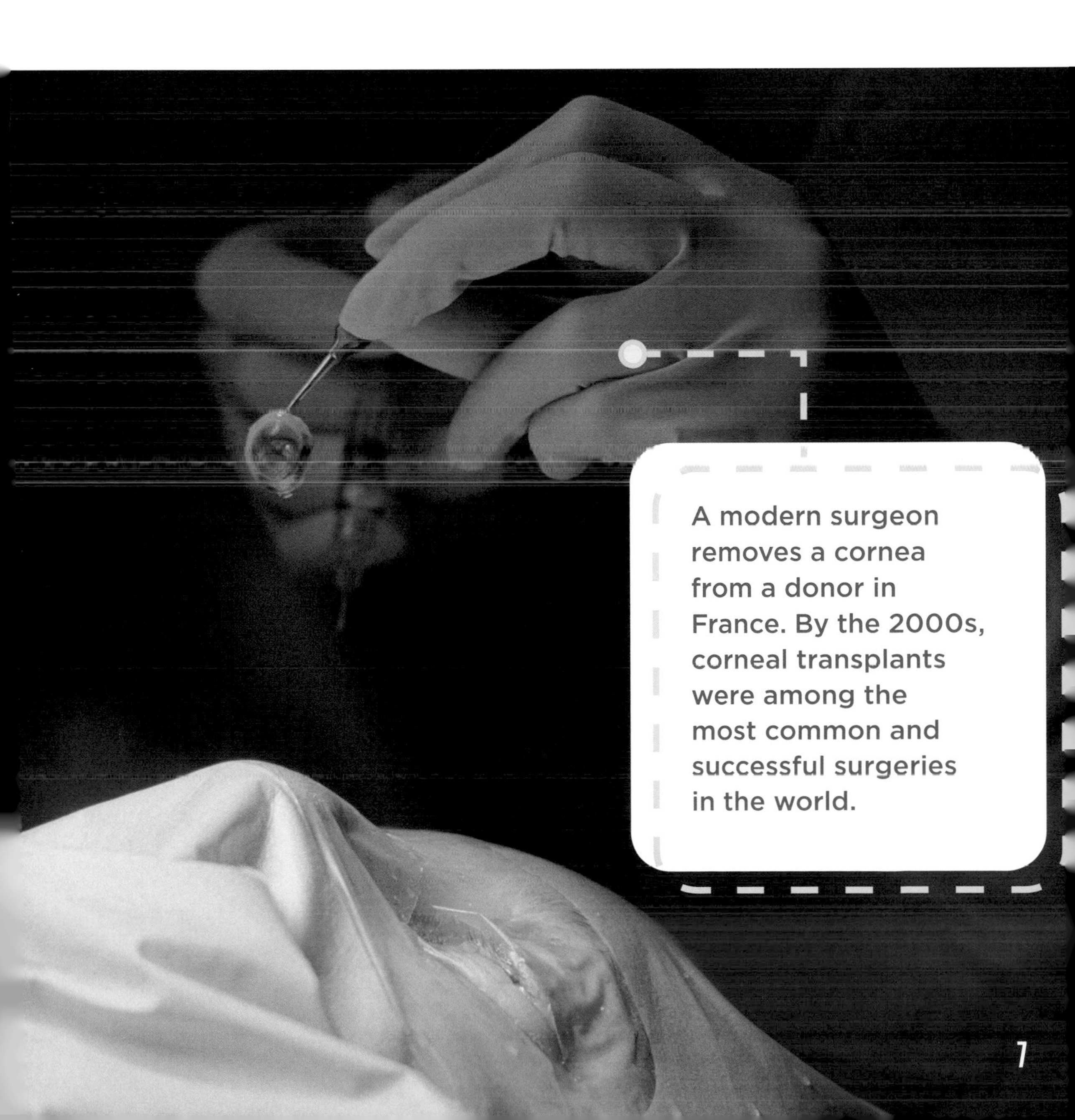

A modern surgeon removes a cornea from a donor in France. By the 2000s, corneal transplants were among the most common and successful surgeries in the world.

THE KEY TO HUMAN ORGAN TRANSPLANT

In 1954, 23-year-old Ronald Herrick wanted to save his twin brother, Richard's, life. Richard suffered from **chronic** kidney failure. Ronald said he would give his brother one of his own kidneys to save him. This sparked an idea in Richard's doctor, David Miller.

By the 1950s, a human-to-human cornea transplant had been successful. But transplanting organs between humans had not been. The human body attacks **foreign** cells. This **immune response** is how the body fights off illness. **Donated** organs are from a foreign body. So the bodies of organ transplant recipients reacted this way to donated organs. An organ transplant would fail in a matter of days or weeks. Sometimes this resulted in the recipient dying.

But Miller thought a transplant between the Herrick brothers just might work. This is because of the brothers' relationship. Being identical twins meant they had the same **genetics**!

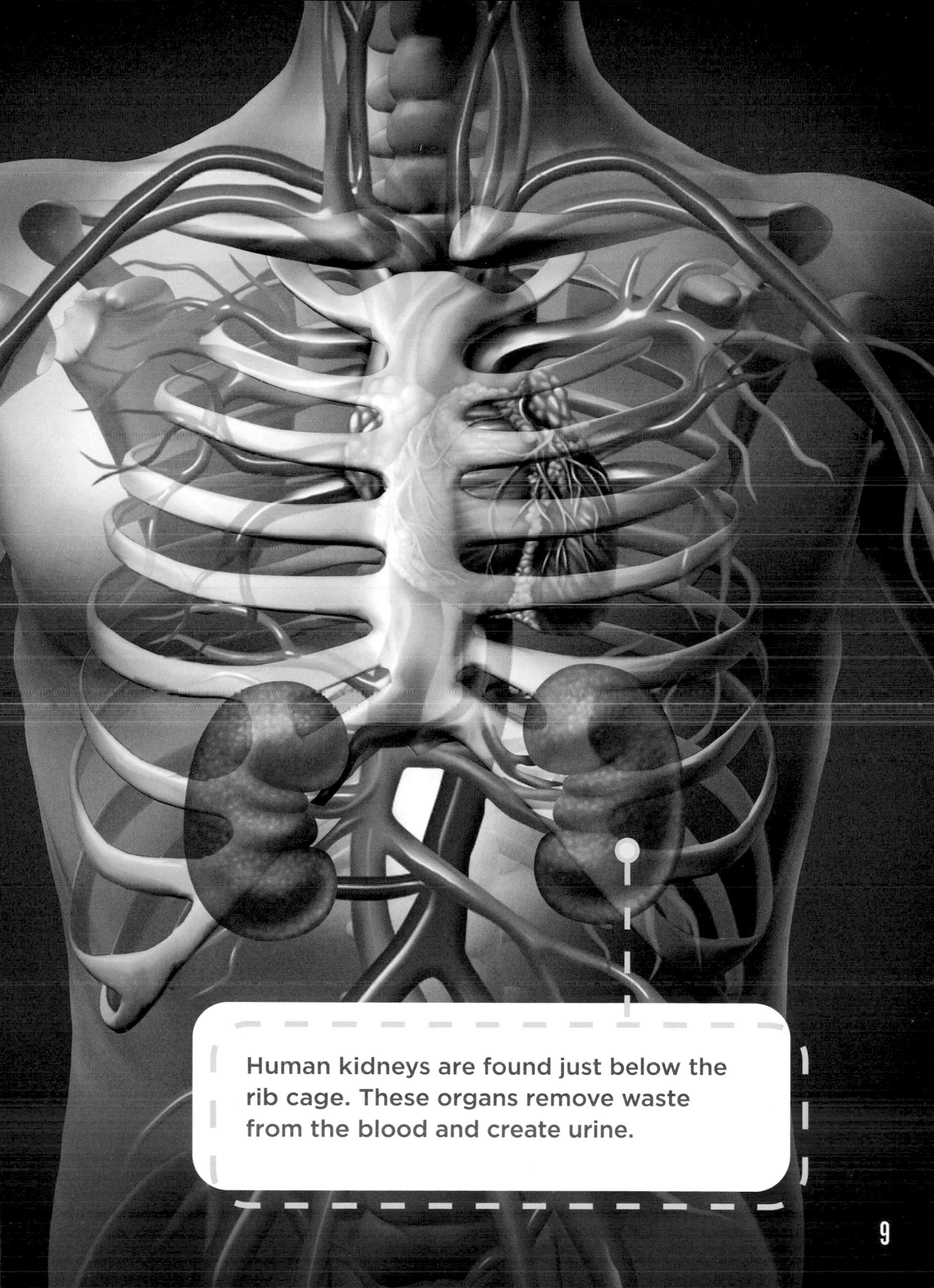
Human kidneys are found just below the rib cage. These organs remove waste from the blood and create urine.

Because the brothers shared genes, Miller believed Richard's body would not recognize Ronald's kidney as foreign.

However, there was another risk to consider. Today, doctors know that humans need only one functioning kidney to survive. But in 1954, this was just a **theory**. Ronald thought about these risks. But he still wanted to go through with the surgery. It was his brother's only chance at life.

Miller performed the surgery on December 23. The brothers survived and both went on to live healthy lives. The operation became famous. It was the world's first successful human-to-human organ transplant!

Today, doctors do several blood tests to successfully match organ recipients and donors. This results in thousands of lifesaving operations. In 2021 alone, nearly 25,000 kidney transplants were performed in the United States.

Richard (*left*) and Ronald (*center*) Herrick exit the Boston, Massachusetts, hospital on January 30, 1955. The twins recovered at the hospital for more than one month following their successful kidney transplant surgeries.

HIGH-TECH TRANSPLANT MATCHING

Doctors learning to successfully match organ donors and recipients changed the medical field. But there were still problems with organ transplants.

Many donations came from people who had recently died. These people had signed forms stating they wanted to donate their organs after death. But organs can't be preserved for long. When an organ became available, it had to be used right away. And it wasn't always easy to find the right recipient match for an available organ. Many organs from recently deceased donors were being wasted.

This changed in 1968. That year, the Southeast Organ Procurement Foundation formed. It used medical information to match donors and recipients.

In 1977, the foundation created the United Network for Organ Sharing (UNOS). This computerized database made matching donors and recipients even easier. The UNOS keeps track of blood type, location, and other information about donors and recipients. It is still in use today and helps donated organs go where they're needed—and quickly!

Human organs are transported in special sterile coolers. They are not unboxed until they reach the operating room during an organ transplant.

WONDER DRUG
CURBS ORGAN REJECTION

Even when doctors make a perfect pairing, a recipient's body might flag a new organ as foreign and **reject** it. In the 1970s, Belgian doctor Jean Borel discovered something to help prevent this.

Borel found the compound cyclosporine could **suppress** the **immune system**. He concluded it could be given as a drug before a transplant. The drug would stop the immune system from flagging foreign objects.

It took time to figure out how to manufacture cyclosporine, and doctors began using the drug in transplants in the 1980s. They gave it to patients four to five hours before surgery. Afterward, patients took the drug every day for the rest of their lives.

The drug helped increase transplant survival rates. However, it could also cause serious side effects. These included an increased risk for developing **infections**. And organ rejection can still occur even when a patient takes cyclosporine.

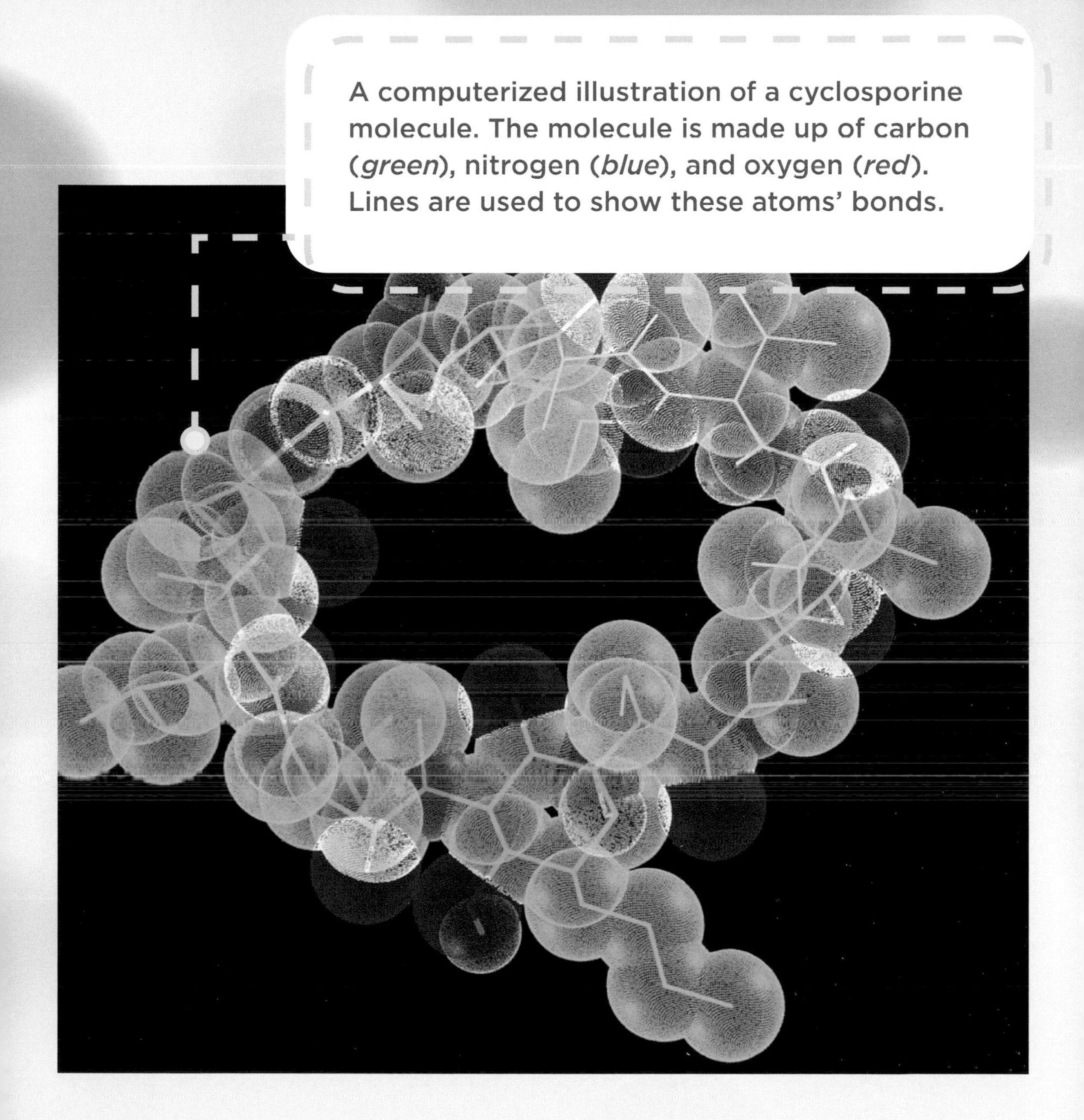

A computerized illustration of a cyclosporine molecule. The molecule is made up of carbon (*green*), nitrogen (*blue*), and oxygen (*red*). Lines are used to show these atoms' bonds.

Even with the side effects, cyclosporine was a big step forward. Following the drug's introduction, more transplants were performed than ever before.

SCIENTIST SPOTLIGHT

SAMAR H. IBRAHIM, MBCHB

MAYO CLINIC

Q: What motivated you to work in adolescent and pediatric medicine?

A: In medical school, I had an interest in the liver and functions of the liver. I wanted to be a pediatrician early in my training and combining my interest in the liver with caring for children seemed to be the right start for me. I chose gastroenterology as my specialty because health and nutrition are the center of care for children. I am fascinated by the complex and essential functions of the liver and interested in watching the lifesaving transformation that liver transplant gives to kids. Nothing is more important

than kids having a normal childhood free from illness, and liver transplant can give them that normal childhood.

Q: What do you wish more people knew about transplants?

A: I wish that more people knew about the gift of life that a transplant provides and would be advocates for transplant and organ donation. We can only transplant the patients on the list with donors, both living and deceased, and I would love to increase awareness about organ donation.

Q: What is the most exciting thing happening in transplant research?

A: Some of the current research includes research to reduce organ waste. When someone makes the decision to donate on the deceased donor list, we want to do everything we can to be able to use that organ. Right now, many of the organs are not perfect, but there are ways to make these organs usable. Future research regarding prevention of immunosuppressive side effects and eventually eliminating these drugs completely is something we all hope will come for patients soon.

BABOON HEART, HUMAN BABY

Stephanie Fae Beauclair was born in 1984 with a fatal heart **defect**. Without a new heart, Stephanie would die. But doctors had never performed a heart transplant on a baby. US surgeon Leonard Bailey wanted to try.

For years, Bailey had experimented transplanting lamb hearts into baby goats, and the goats survived. He thought baboons may be genetically close enough to humans to allow successful transplants. And now Bailey thought his research might help save baby Stephanie.

On October 26, 1984, Bailey transplanted the heart from a baby baboon into Stephanie. The heart saved her life for three weeks. But then, Stephanie's body rejected the heart and she died.

Bailey's surgery created controversy. Some people thought it was unfair to the baboon. Others praised Bailey for trying to find new treatments. Either way, Bailey's surgery raised awareness about the need for infant organ donation.

An illustration shows the differences between a typical human heart, baby Stephanie's heart, and a baboon heart. Human hearts have three arteries connected to a curving arch, while baboon hearts have only two. Bailey left much of Stephanie's arteries in place and opened the baboon's arch. Then he sewed the arteries and arch together.

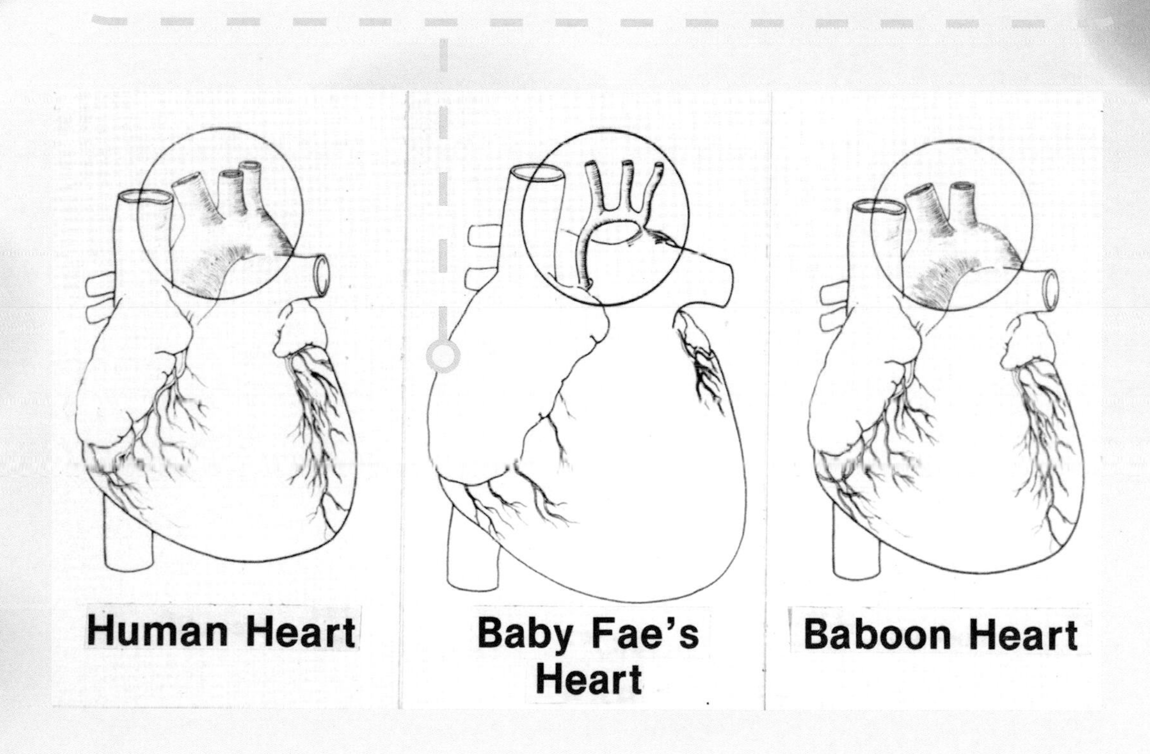

A year later, Bailey performed a human-to-human heart transplant on baby Eddie Anguiano. Eddie survived long term. Bailey had performed the first successful infant heart transplant! Modern heart transplants save the lives of 600 to 700 babies worldwide each year.

MODIFIED AND LAB-GROWN ORGANS

By the late 1980s, doctors knew how to perform transplants. But there weren't enough donors. Many people believed myths about donation. Some believed if they were a donor and needed medical care, doctors would not work to save their lives, instead stealing their organs for other patients!

To solve donor shortages, scientists continued brainstorming animal-human transplants. In the 1990s, they learned pig and human organs were similar. The scientists researched genetically **modifying** pigs to make their organs **viable** for human transplant.

Research continued for decades. In 2022, US doctors operated on David Bennett, a man with fatal heart disease. Bennett received a genetically modified pig heart. He lived for two months with it! Animal-human transplants have not provided long-term survival. But some doctors think any extra time gives patients a chance of a human donation becoming available.

In addition to organ modification, scientists researched growing organs. In 2006, doctors at North Carolina's Wake Forest

University School of Medicine took **tissue** from seven patients who needed bladder transplants. They used the tissue to grow bladders. Transplanting the grown bladders was successful! Scientists and doctors worldwide were inspired to try growing transplant kidneys, livers, and hearts.

A bladder grows inside a beaker and incubator at Harvard Medical School in Massachusetts. The bladder has been growing for five weeks. It will be ready for transplant at around 12 weeks.

STEM CELL SUCCESS

By 2022, using cyclosporine to prevent organ rejection had become common in transplants. But the drug's side effects made many doctors hope for another option. That year, doctors at California's Stanford University leapt toward that goal. The doctors used a special method to perform kidney transplants on three children. The children's parents acted as donors!

First, doctors removed **stem cells** from a parent and **implanted** them into the child. This allowed the child's immune system to recognize cells from the parent. Over the next two to three months, the child's immune system would become **compatible** with these cells. This would prepare the child's body to accept the donated organ.

On the day of the transplant surgery, doctors removed the donated kidney from a parent and transplanted it into the child—without the use of any anti-rejection drugs. The bodies of all three children accepted the kidneys long-term.

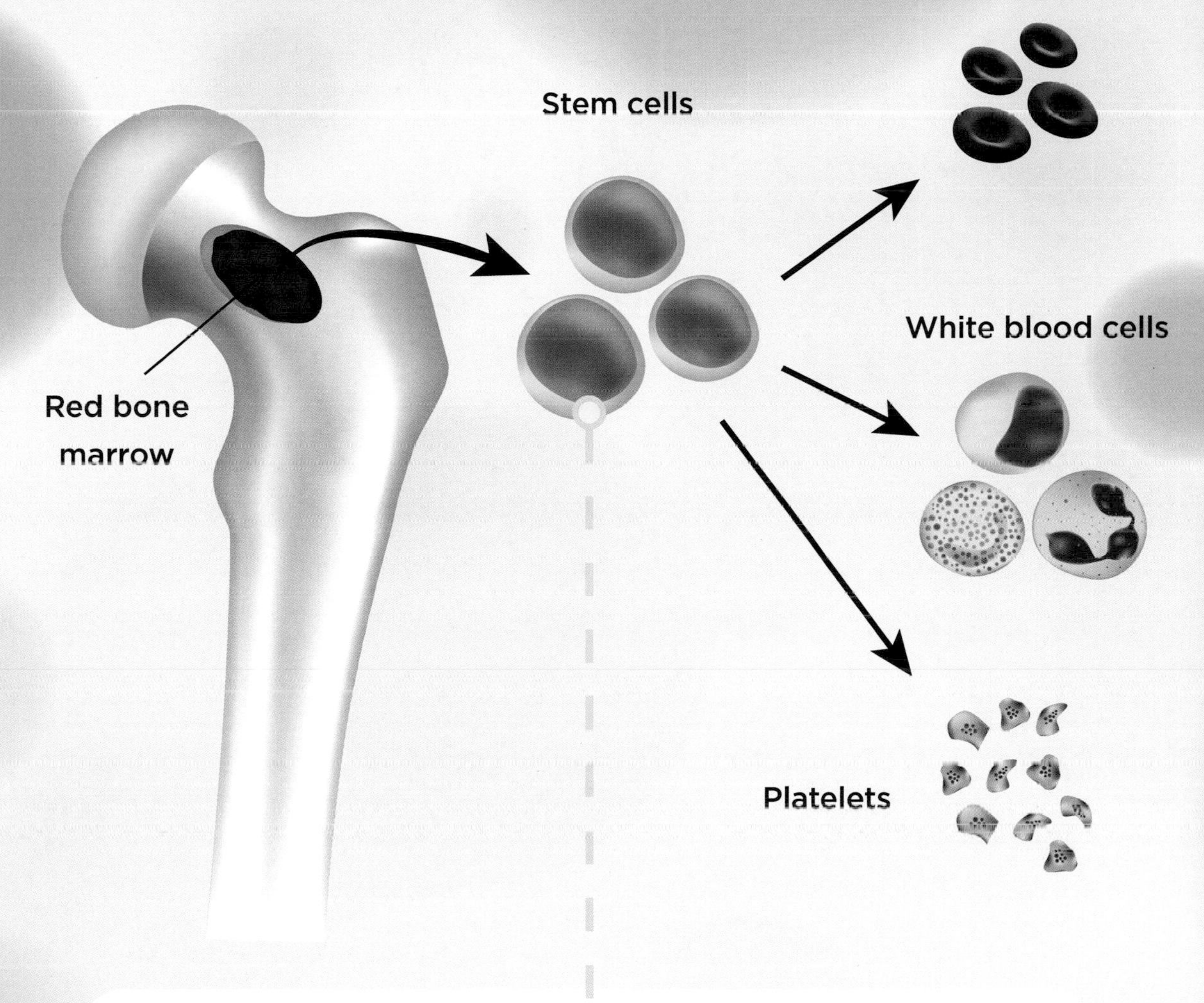

Stem cells from adults are often taken from their red bone marrow. This tissue is in the center of most bones and is where blood cells develop. Stem cells have not yet formed into blood cells. When they fully form, they become either red blood cells, white blood cells, or platelets. When stem cells are removed from a donor and then transplanted, this formation happens in the recipient's body.

ICE-COLD ORGANS

Doctors have no time to waste when transplanting organs. Kidneys can only be outside the body for 24 to 36 hours. A liver must be transplanted within 8 to 12 hours of removal, and a heart within 4 to 6 hours. Medical teams hoped to preserve donated organs for longer. In 2022, Minnesota's Mayo Clinic and the University of Minnesota (U of M) found a way!

The medical teams used **cryopreservation** to store pancreatic **islet cells**. These may be a cure for **diabetes**. They last 48 to 72 hours outside the body. This is longer than other organs. But pancreatic islet recipients need cells from many donors for the transplant to work. Gathering these cells takes time. So, patients receiving this type of transplant had to have several surgeries.

To give doctors more time to gather these cells, the Mayo and U of M teams cryopreserve them. The low temperatures prevent cell **decay**. When the cells are rewarmed, they can be transplanted into patients. This process allows for transplanting cells from many donors in just one surgery.

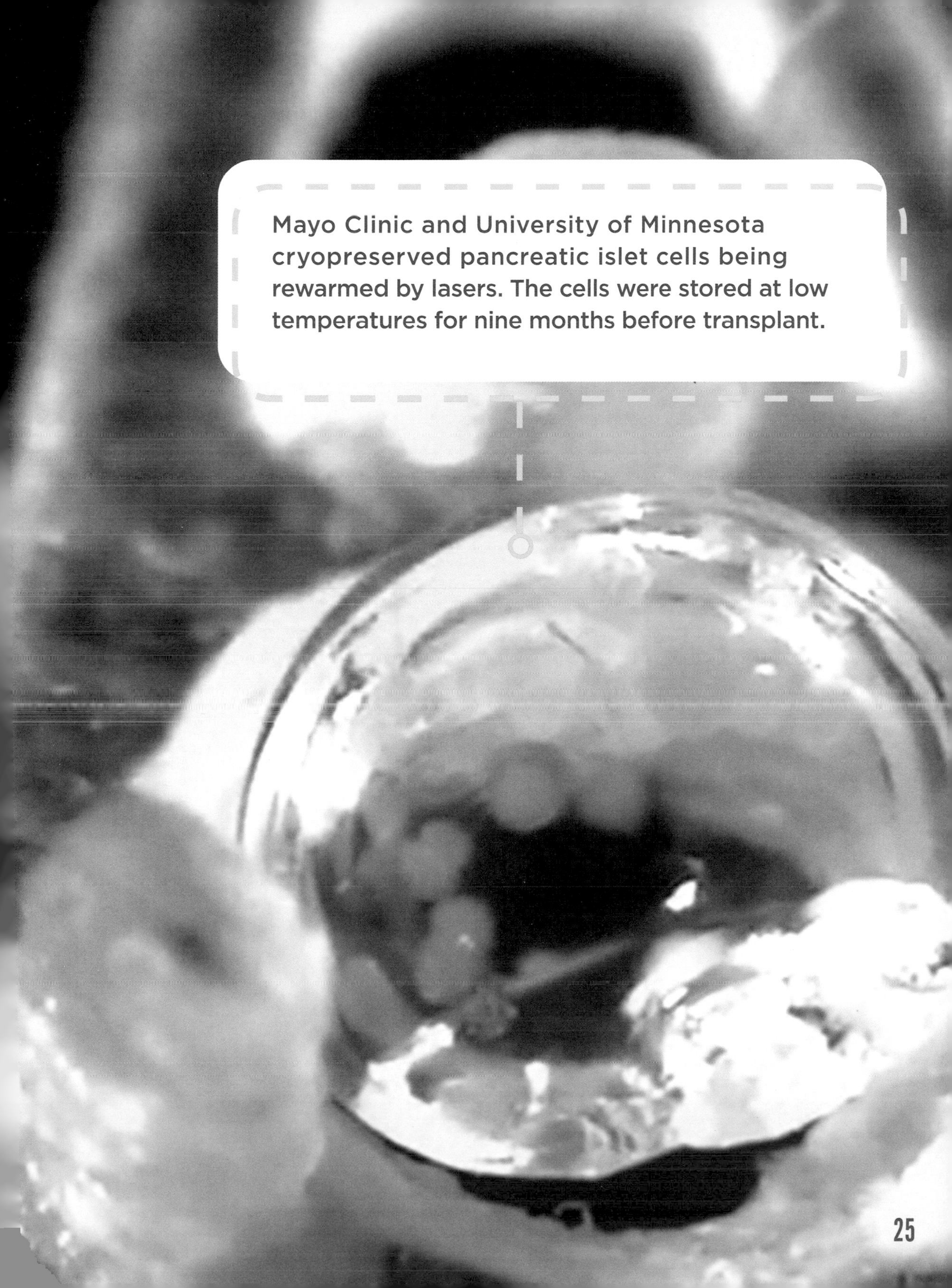

Mayo Clinic and University of Minnesota cryopreserved pancreatic islet cells being rewarmed by lasers. The cells were stored at low temperatures for nine months before transplant.

BIOPRINTING
BRINGS NEW HOPE

Imagine a world where finding organs for people in need was no problem, even if there weren't enough donors. Researchers at US company United Therapeutics think 3D bioprinting could make this possible! Bioprinting is 3D printing using living cells. In 2022, United Therapeutics bioprinted lungs for animals. Human recipients could be next!

At Mayo Clinic in Arizona, the use of 3D-printed human body parts already began in 2021. The clinic printed **larynx** implants. The implants replaced larynx tissue that had been removed due to **cancer** or injury. Mayo scientists were also exploring how to 3D print an entire larynx implant.

Nearly 106,000 people were on the US national transplant waiting list in 2022. Medical 3D printing could create organs for some recipients. Inventors continue to draw on past research and think outside the box in exploring transplant technology. Their breakthroughs can help transplants of the future be safer, simpler, and more successful!

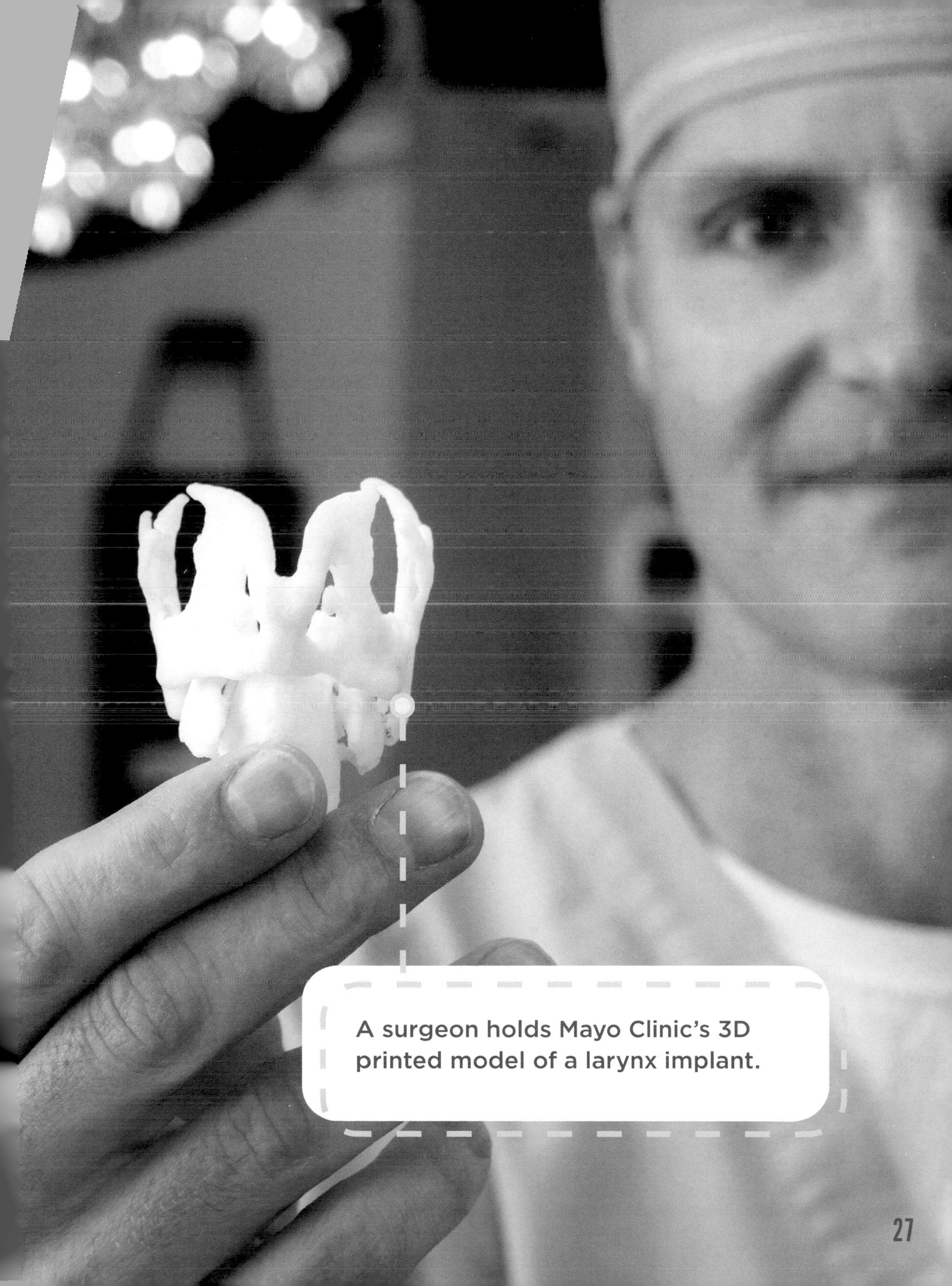

A surgeon holds Mayo Clinic's 3D printed model of a larynx implant.

TIMELINE

1905

Eduard Zirm performs the first successful corneal transplant.

1954

Ronald Herrick donates his kidney to his twin brother, Richard. It is the first successful living donor kidney transplant. This teaches doctors that matching blood types is key to transplant success.

1977

The United Network for Organ Sharing is created. It keeps track of medical information to match organ donors and recipients more easily.

1980s

Doctors begin giving transplant recipients cyclosporine in preparation for surgery. Its success in preventing organ rejection leads to more successful transplants.

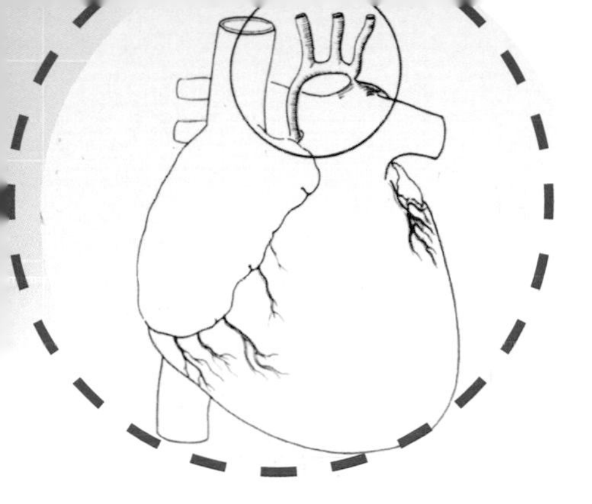

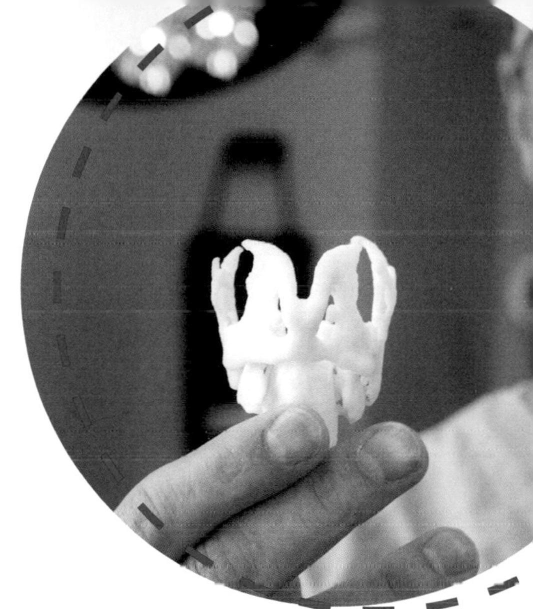

1984

Infant Stephanie Fae Beauclair lives for three weeks with a transplanted baboon heart.

2021

Mayo Clinic doctors use 3D printing to create larynx tissue implants.

2006

Scientists grow bladders in a lab and successfully transplant them into people.

2022

Three child patients receive dual donations of stem cells and then kidneys from one of their parents. The process eliminates the need for cyclosporine, sparing the children from the drug's side effects.

Mayo Clinic and University of Minnesota researchers develop a cryopreservation storage for pancreatic islet cells.

GLOSSARY

cancer—a group of often deadly diseases in which harmful cells spread quickly

chronic—continuing or occurring again and again for a long time

compatible—able to exist or work together well

controversy—a dispute or debate marked by opposing views. Topics of these debates are called controversial.

cornea—the clear outer covering of the eyeball. Something relating to the cornea is called corneal.

cryopreserve—to preserve by keeping at a low temperature. This process is called cryopreservation.

decay—decline in health or strength

defect—a lack of something essential

diabetes—a condition that affects how the body processes sugar

donate—to give something in order to help. A person who donates is called a donor and the thing they give is called a donation.

foreign—something that is not a part of, or is from outside, the body

gene—the smallest unit of characteristics passed from parent to offspring. The study of genes is called genetics. Things relating to genes are genetic.

immune response—how the immune system reacts to changes or foreign objects

immune system—the body's system that fights off disease and infection

implant—to place something in a person's body during surgery. The item placed is also called an implant.

infection—the entrance and growth of germs in the body

islet cell—a pancreatic cell that produces hormones that are discharged into the bloodstream

larynx—a hollow muscular organ located in the neck, and which allows humans to speak and swallow

modify—to make changes to. These changed items are called modified and the changes are called modifications.

permanent—lasting forever

reject—to not accept. This act is called rejection.

stem cells—cells that can develop into many different types of cells

suppress—to slow or stop normal functioning

surgery—a medical treatment performed on internal body parts. This treatment is performed by a surgeon.

theory—a group of ideas meant to explain something

tissue—a group of like cells that work together in the body to perform a function

viable—capable of being used

LEARN MORE

Britannica Kids: Transplant
https://kids.britannica.com/kids/article/transplant/390865

Kenney, Karen Latchana. *Cutting-Edge 3D Printing*. Minneapolis: Lerner Publishing Group, 2018.

Mayo Clinic: Transplant Center
https://www.mayoclinic.org/departments-centers/transplant-center/home/orc-20203891

National Institute of Environmental Health Sciences: Scientific Method
https://kids.niehs.nih.gov/topics/how-science-works/scientific-method/index.htm

Organ Transplants: What Every Kid Needs to Know. Richmond, Virginia: United Network for Organ Sharing, 2020. https://unos.org/wp-content/uploads/Brochure-113k-What-every-kid-needs-to-know.pdf

INDEX

PHOTO ACKNOWLEDGMENTS

Akarawut Lohacharoenvanich/iStockphoto, cover (surgery); Alfred Pasieka/Science Source, p. 15; Alila Medical Media/Shutterstock Images, p. 23; anusorn nakdee/iStockphoto, cover (stem cells); AP Images, pp. 11, 19, 28, 29 (left); artoleshko/iStockphoto, cover (heart); Lightspring/Shutterstock Images, p. 9; Mayo Clinic, back cover, pp. 16, 27, 29 (right); Michelle Del Guercio/Science Source, p. 13; Rajau/Science Source, p. 7; Sam Ogden/Science Source, p. 21; TommyStockProject/Shutterstock Images, cover (child patient and doctor); traffic_analyzer/iStockphoto, cover (background); University Of Maryland School Of Medicine/ZUMA Press, Inc./Alamy, p. 5; Zhan, L., Rao, J.S., Sethia, N. et al., University of Minnesota, p. 25